Temple by the Sea

a novel by
Jamila Gavin

The Temple by the Sea

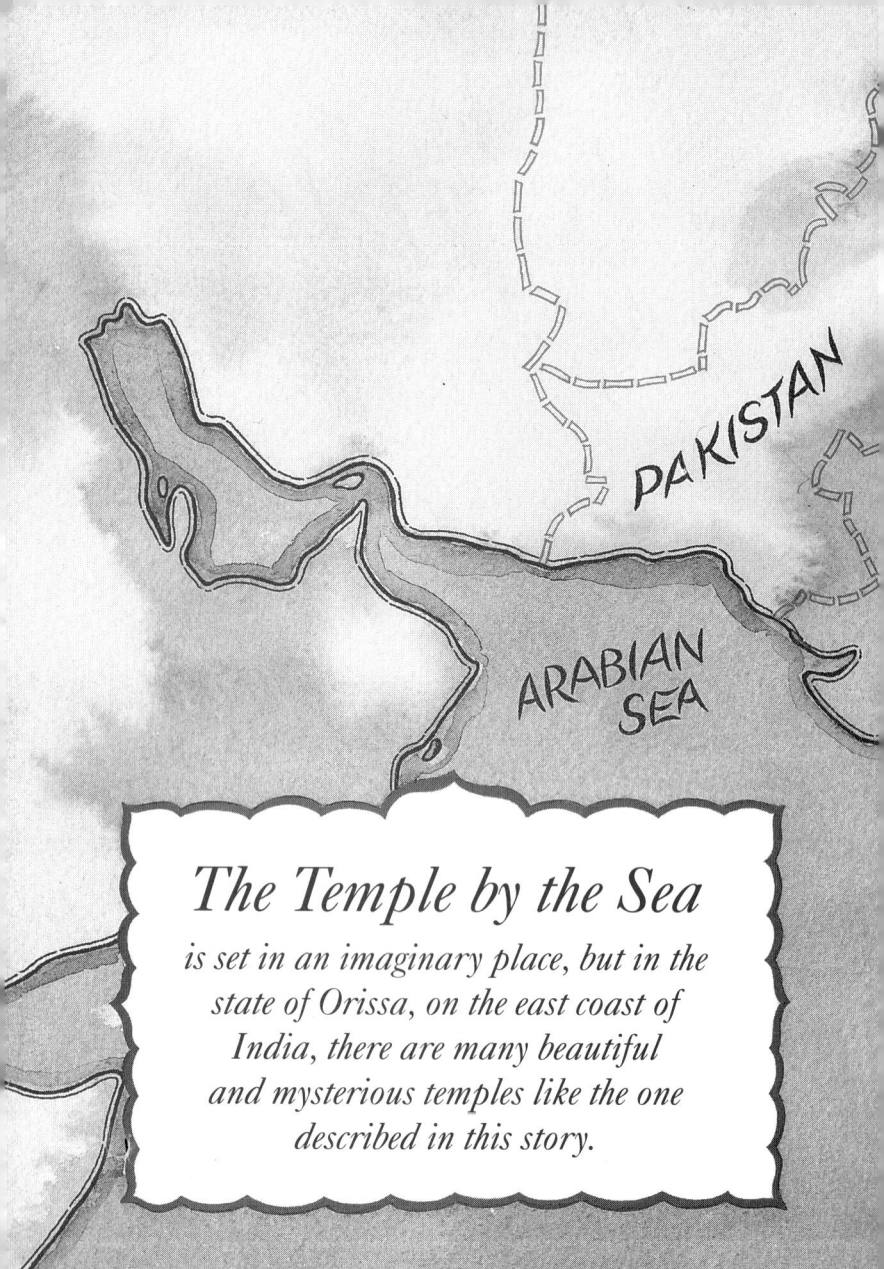

is set in an imaginary place, but in the state of Orissa, on the east coast of India, there are many beautiful and mysterious temples like the one described in this story.

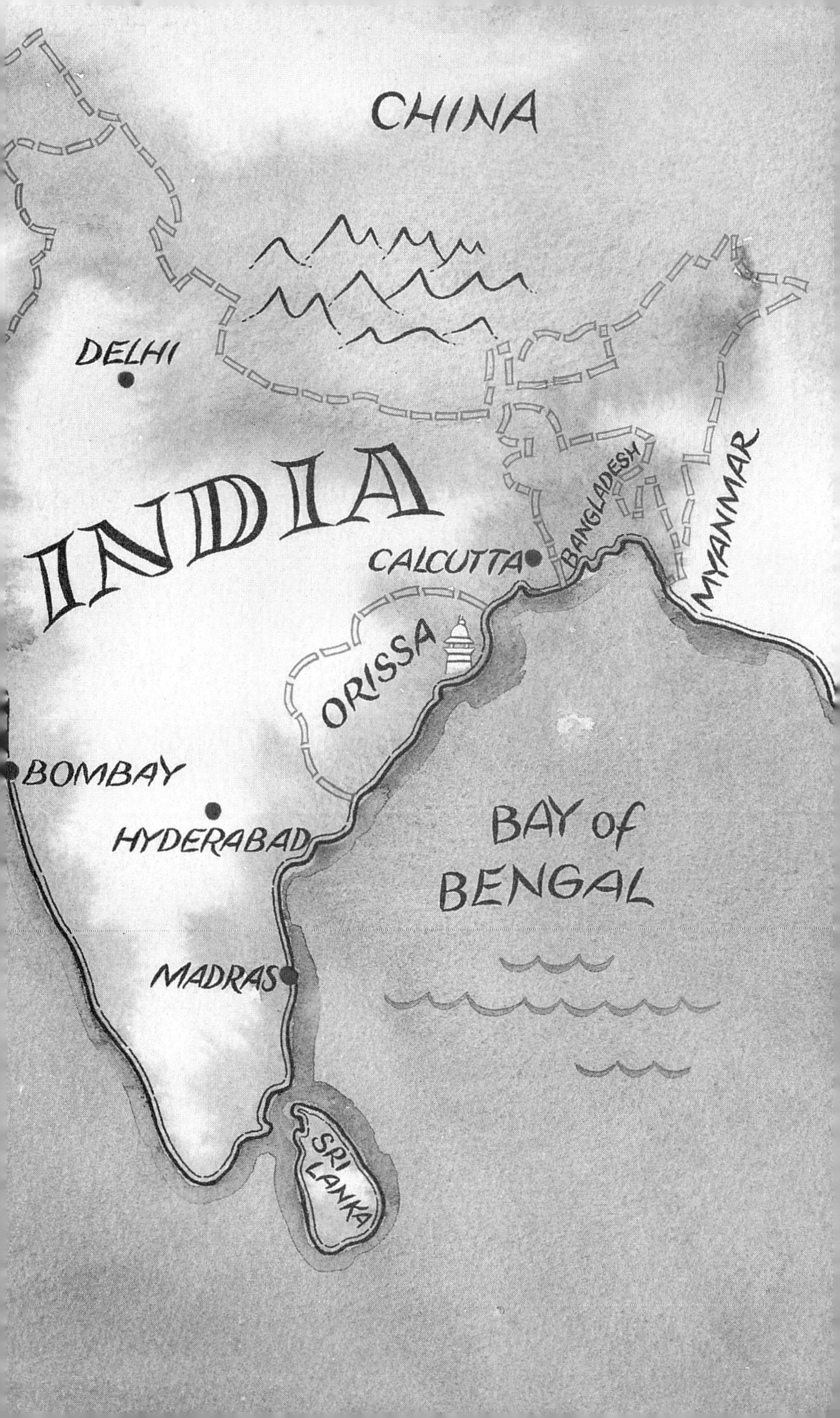

CHINA
DELHI
INDIA
CALCUTTA
BANGLADESH
MYANMAR
ORISSA
BOMBAY
HYDERABAD
BAY of
BENGAL
MADRAS
SRI
LANKA

*The words
underlined in the text
are defined in the glossary
on page 78.*

CHAPTER 1
The Lonely Temple

There is an empty stretch of coastline which runs like a bleak lonely thread alongside the Indian Ocean. No one seems to go there, except for a few brave fishermen in their shallow open boats which are no more than one or two logs tied together. Each morning they risk their lives taking their nets far, far out to cast into the dangerous seas. Each evening they return with their catch – sometimes so <u>meagre</u> it could hardly feed a family – and plunge into the treacherous waves to drag their craft ashore before the great curtain of night closes on the sun.

Behind the coast, the fringe of jungle is still quite thick, although not much of it is left now; for behind it, the farmers have cleared the earth, carving out more space to grow crops. They have no time for looking at the sea. Life is too hard. All day long they toil, guiding the plough, sowing the seed, watering the soil and then reaping the crop.

But once a year, they all turn their faces to the sea. Once a year they build a huge <u>effigy</u> of the goddess Kali, moulded out of clay and held together with sticks and straw. She is painted black, with fearful, wide, blood-shot eyes and a great tongue, which hangs out of her mouth dripping blood. The priests dress her in a glittering <u>sari</u> and drape her in pearls and precious stones. Then, with loud banging of drums, clashing of bells and the heart-piercing shriek of reed pipes, they parade their effigy through the village, across the fields and down to the old ruined temple by the sea, to unite her with her husband – Lord Shiva.

No one knows how old the temple is. It has been there throughout all memory and before. Its great granite <u>edifice</u> rises up like a chariot. Every inch of the hard grey stone is carved as finely and delicately as lace, with figures that leap and dance and work and play and love and die. It has wide terraces all around, with arches and columns carefully designed so that the rising sun appears exactly through the middle at dawn, and sets in perfect symmetry on the other side.

It was here on these very stones, people claim, that Lord Shiva danced his dance of the <u>Cosmos</u>. And it was here that over the centuries, pilgrims, especially dancers, had travelled from all over India to pay homage to the great Lord Shiva. They would worship before the Destroyer of Evil, whose dancing feet crushed demons and whose whirling arms <u>annihilated</u> his enemies. The rhythm of Lord Shiva's dance is the heart-beat of the universe, and the pilgrims hoped that if they too danced on those same stones, the cosmic power would come up through the soles of their feet and they would dance like gods.

Then there was an earthquake – not in living memory, but over two hundred years ago. Some said Shiva got angry – but others insisted that it was his wife, the goddess Kali. They said she had become jealous of those dancers who had come to steal some of Lord Shiva's cosmic power.

Whatever the reason, some force had dragged the temple right into the waves – so that now, even to this day, it is half in and half out of the sea.

From then on, a terrible legend grew around the temple. It was said that if any dancer came to dance on those ancient sacred stones, she would be cursed. It was said that the earthquake had released all the sorrows of the world; that the pain of all the souls of those who had died in torment would pass through into the feet of the dancer. Although that dancer would now dance as wonderfully as Lord Shiva himself, it would only last for a while – and then either the pain would drive the dancer mad, or she would wish she could have her feet chopped off to relieve the agony.

At first, the dancers still kept coming. There was always someone who laughed at the legend or thought it would be worth the chance of being the best dancer in the world – thought it would be worth risking Kali's displeasure to gain Lord Shiva's divine gift.

It was said that the Keeper of the Temple was grief-stricken at the loss of so many talented dancers. And he was terrified that one day Kali would again show her anger and try to destroy what was left of their precious temple. So he made a secret pact with the great goddess. It is said that one evening before sunset, he stepped on to the accursed terrace and walked down its ruined slope into the sea. He tied himself to a half-submerged pillar to stop himself being swept away and all through the night he prayed.

The priests on the shore were certain they would never see him alive again. They saw the giant waves curling around him like serpents and they heard the voices of the drowned, gurgling up from the depths and shrieking into the wind.

All night long, the priests chanted hymns as loudly as they could to give the keeper courage. When finally the dawn light came spreading across the eastern sky, they walked silently through the ruins to the edge of the sea. They had expected to retrieve his body, but instead, they found that the keeper had untied himself and was walking back towards the temple. His face was serene and seemed to glow with a strange secret.

"It is done," was all he would say.

CHAPTER 2
The Dream

Far away over the ocean from the temple by the sea, far away in England, lived a girl called Shanta.

The day Shanta decided she wanted to be a dancer was on her cousin Rani Shankar's thirteenth birthday.

A lavish party had been organized, for Rani's parents doted on their daughter. They were convinced she was the most beautiful and talented girl in the world – and that, soon, she would be known as the greatest dancer of her time. How they enjoyed showing her off.

Being extremely wealthy, the Shankars never did anything by halves. They lived in a large house, drove large cars, sent their children to the most expensive schools, and paid anything that was necessary to ensure that their only daughter, Rani, had the best teachers and musicians to instruct her in music and dance.

But though they were rich, they were very generous and loved to have their house full of people. They loved celebrations and often threw parties – it didn't matter whether it was for birthdays or anniversaries, <u>Divali</u> or even Christmas.

Rani's birthday was always considered a very special occasion. People looked forward to it, because everyone came, from the youngest to the oldest. Cousins and aunts and uncles and grannies and grandpas, and all Rani's friends from school – they all came. There would be mountains of food and rivers of wine and fruit juices; and a constant <u>caravan</u> of dishes would parade through with all sorts of savouries and titbits and delicious sweets. Although the Shankars always brought in the finest entertainers to amuse their many party guests, it was Rani herself who would be the star performer, rounding off the evening with a brilliant demonstration of her dancing.

Ever since Rani's birthday invitation had arrived, Shanta's mother, Mrs Biswas, had been fretting about what to wear. Mrs Biswas often wore an expression of annoyance. She was mostly annoyed because she felt her parents had made her marry beneath her. Mr Biswas was a teacher and would never be rich – not like Mr Shankar, Rani's father, who was in business. Mrs Biswas envied the Shankars' large house and big cars; and she especially envied the beautiful saris Mr Shankar brought back for his wife whenever he went off on a business trip.

However, every party invitation was received eagerly – for it would be terrible not to be included on the Shankar party list, even though it meant terrible anxiety about what to wear. Mrs Biswas dreaded looking poorer than the rest. She would flick through the saris which hung in her wardrobe and then conclude in a very loud voice, for the benefit of her husband, "I have nothing to wear. I'll just have to go shopping."

"Why can't you wear that one of Banarasi silk which I bought you on our last visit to India?" asked Shanta's father in a pained voice.

"Because I wore that at the Mahajans' party, and everyone would remember it," retorted his wife, who could never be seen at a party in the same sari twice.

"I think you should wear that beautiful turquoise blue one with the peacock border," murmured Shanta.

"Don't be silly, child," pouted her mother, annoyed. "That's not good enough for a party at the Shankars'." She looked at her daughter and couldn't help showing her irritation. The girl was so awkward, so nondescript; so unpretty. Shanta's mother had never forgotten overhearing one of her sisters-in-law making the comment that if one must have daughters, at least they should be pretty.

"It's too bad," Shanta's mother often groaned. "Why should the Shankars have wealth as well as beauty?" She thought of her niece, Rani, with her fair skin, slender figure and face like a goddess, and compared her to Shanta. In her opinion, Shanta's skin was too dark, her forehead too broad, her feet too big and her figure rather stumpy. True, she had large glowing eyes, and people said of Shanta that her eyes and her rich black hair were her most beautiful features; but where would eyes get you in this world? Who would want to marry her? Shanta's mother gave a discontented sigh. "I suppose we had better decide what you are going to wear, too," she said to her daughter.

"I shall wear the <u>shalwar kameez</u> which Dad brought me back from India," said Shanta. "It's really lovely."

The day of the party came round. That morning, when Shanta woke up, she felt a strange excitement stirring in her. She wondered why. She had been to parties before, so why, this time, did she feel a curious tightening in her chest – a kind of nervous excitement, as if something extraordinary was going to happen?

She got out of bed and looked in the mirror. It wasn't *her* birthday, but she felt different. She examined herself. No – there was the same old face and the same old body on the outside. Yet inside, her blood was racing and her feet were tingling. She stamped a dancer's stamp and twisted her hands as a dancer does. Her heart was beating fast like a tabla drum and she thought she heard a voice inside her head murmuring the dancer's rhythm, "Thakka-dhimi-thakka-jhanu-thakka-dhimi-thakka-jhanu!"

Then she remembered her dream. She had dreamt she was dancing in a strange temple. As she danced, she noticed that the stone walls were carved with figures of dancers. Their limbs twisted and flowed like the branches of trees, yet their <u>torsos</u> were as solid as the rock into which they were carved. You could almost hear the ankle bells jingling as they stamped their feet, and the rattle of tablas from the stone musicians who sat in attendance.

Suddenly, in her dream, the dancers came alive and leapt out of the rock. They surrounded her, urging her to dance too. But then the dream turned into a nightmare, for as the dance ended, she felt herself being drawn back into the rock with them and her body turned to stone. When she woke up and thought about it, she wondered if it was worth being turned to stone by day, if by night you could come alive and dance. For Shanta longed to dance more than anything. How she wished she was more like Rani.

CHAPTER 3
The Mysterious Tabla Player

When they arrived at the party, Shanta's mother and father were immediately swept away into a glittering crowd of grown-ups. Rani's mother told Shanta to go and play with the other children out in the garden.

Was Rani out there too, Shanta wondered? Although Rani was three years older than her, they had become friends when Shanta had come to stay with the Shankars one summer, while her parents went back to India on a visit. The two girls liked doing the same things: they both loved dressing up and acting and dancing. They used to take it in turns to drum and sing while the other danced. They learned all the stories about Lord Krishna and the milkmaids and how he used to tease them, and how he really loved Radha, the most beautiful of all the milkmaids. Sometimes Rani and Shanta danced before their family and friends, and this was how Rani's parents decided their daughter was really talented and should go and have proper dancing lessons. When Shanta begged her mother and father to let her go too, there always seemed to be an excuse. First she was too young, then the lessons were too expensive, then there wasn't really time – and anyway, she wasn't beautiful and talented like Rani, so it would be better to concentrate on something else. So Shanta, who had a cassette player in her room, used to content herself by dancing secretly to her music tapes and pretending that she was one of those dancers she saw from time to time in Hindi films.

At last Shanta saw her cousin at the far end of the crowded room. She wasn't outside playing with the other children, she was helping her mother to be a hostess, by passing round plates of <u>samosas</u> and taking away empty glasses to fill them up again. Shanta wanted to rush over and say hello – but suddenly she felt shy. Rani no longer looked like a child. She seemed to have grown taller since they last met. She was wearing the most elegant shalwar kameez of palest blue and silver. Her face was made up delicately, with powder and lipstick and a flush of <u>rouge</u> on her cheeks, and her eyes were outlined with black. Between her eyebrows was a simple red <u>tilak</u> and her black hair was gathered up into one plait and strewn with pearls. She looked so grown up.

Sadly, Shanta stepped through the French windows on to a smooth lawn. She could see the other children; they pranced about at the other end of the garden, confident, noisy and challenging, and she didn't feel like joining them. Somewhere, she thought she could hear the beat of a tabla. It seemed to be coming from an upstairs window so, when no one was looking, she slipped back inside the house and climbed the stairs, following the sound to the second floor.

The drumming grew louder; its beat was like a magnet and drew her closer and closer to it. Suddenly she found herself standing outside a door. How she could dare to open it she did not know, but as if in a dream, her hand took the knob and silently turned it. The door opened. The drumming rushed out loudly, so she hurriedly stepped into the room and shut the door behind her.

The curtains were drawn and the room was darkened. A heavy rich smell of <u>incense</u> filled her nostrils and she saw the drummer seated cross-legged in a far corner with a pair of tablas, one under each hand. He had his back to her as he played, facing a small altar, in the centre of which was a dark iron statue of a god in a dancing pose. At first she though it was Lord Shiva, Lord of the Dance; but then she saw the necklace of severed heads, the whirling axe, the tongue hanging out and a ferocious tiger leaping behind, and she knew it was the goddess Kali, dancing on the bodies of demons.

On one side of the goddess was an incense stick, its tip glowing red in the darkness and a thin coil of grey scented smoke rising to the ceiling. On the other side was a shallow saucer in which burned a thin flame. Laid before the goddess was a half coconut and an offering of rice and spices.

Suddenly the drummer stopped playing. Shanta froze, terrified. She felt like a spy. She would have turned and fled from the room, but she was rooted to the spot.

The drummer changed from his sitting position and knelt low before the altar with his hands clasped in prayer. He murmured some words, lifted the saucer with the flame and circled it several times in the air before the statue. Then he replaced the saucer, tipped water from a bronze jug into the palm of his hand and tossed it over the fearsome Kali. When he had murmured more prayers, he returned to his cross-legged position and began to play again. He never turned and saw Shanta so, as his drum beats hammered into the air, she quietly opened the door and made her escape, glad that she had not been seen or heard.

For a while, she wandered about, nibbling whatever took her fancy and playing with the little ones who rolled and tumbled among the party guests. Then she noticed that Rani had disappeared, and she heard someone say that she had gone to change into her dancing costume.

At last, everyone was told to gather in the living room, where lots of chairs, sofas and floor cushions had been placed in a semi-circle. Everyone made themselves comfortable and waited, murmuring with expectation. Shanta settled herself into a window seat at the side, and suddenly felt that same tremor of excitement surge through her. It was a nervous excitement, almost as if she herself were about to perform in front of all these people. Her fingers and toes were tingling and her heart was hammering.

There was a burst of applause as the same tabla player whom Shanta had seen earlier entered the room. She heard an awed whisper. "Why, look! That's Mohan Datt, the master tabla player."

He was a short, dark man; thin, yet powerful. He had the face of a hawk soaring in flight – distant, yet watching with microscopic eye.

He wore a pure white Indian shirt and white pyjamas, with a dark red shawl slung around his shoulders. Walking at his master's side was a young disciple, a boy about Shanta's age. The boy was blind, although it was not immediately apparent for he walked as though he hardly needed the hand on his elbow that lightly guided him. The master tabla player sat the boy down on a carpet before a wooden, stringed, long-necked musical instrument – a tanpura – which was for strumming very quietly as a drone. The Master then turned and, with clasped hands, bowed and greeted the audience with a namaste. It was the first time Shanta had seen the tabla player's face clearly – and it made her feel uneasy. His eyes roved over all the faces waiting expectantly before him, yet without really seeing them – until he turned his eyes on Shanta. Then he looked at her hard and long, and seemed to give her an extra special namaste all to herself. It was as though he recognized her. Shanta shivered. Had he known, after all, that she had entered his room while he was praying?

The sound of jingling ankle bells heralded Rani's entrance. Everyone gasped when they saw how magnificent she looked in her dancing costume of scarlet and gold. They clapped and smiled with enthusiasm as she greeted everyone with a namaste, and bowed before the tabla player. He bowed low in return, then sat cross-legged before his drums, one under each hand. Rani took up her position in the middle of the room and stood, still as a statue, waiting till everyone was settled.

The blind boy plucked the strings of the tanpura and a low note, like bees humming, resonated round the room. The drummer struck the skin of the tabla with a hard flat finger. It was like a single heart beat. He struck it again and then he struck the other drum. Now he began to play a slow beat. Rani listened, motionless. Then she moved her eyes in rhythm, looking from one side to the other; she lifted her eyebrows as if she were thinking magical thoughts; without moving from the spot, her foot took up the rhythm and tapped with a beat while her shoulders undulated.

From the back of the room, Shanta watched. She was entranced. The rhythm made her soul shiver. Her eye caught the eye of the tabla player; he seemed to be beating the drum for her. Shanta slipped unnoticed out of her seat and, as if hypnotized, began to move with the beat.

At the front, Rani glowed like a sparkling flower. Her beauty dazzled, her movements were so graceful. Everyone's eyes were on her, smiling with pleasure, so they didn't see how Shanta danced. Shanta danced and danced, forgetting where she was, her ears only hearing the liquid beat of the tabla and her body turning from that of a stumpy child into a gracefully moving figure, like a temple statue come to life. Her face was transformed so that she no longer looked like that little girl her mother thought so "unpretty". There was a look on her face as if she had glimpsed paradise – and it made her the most beautiful person in the room, if only anyone had bothered to look.

Rani entered the climax of her dance, whirling round faster and faster and faster with her long plait flying, her skirt spread out like a spinning top and the bells on her feet jingling like galloping horses. Then, with a joyful flourish, she came to a stop, her face flushed and beads of perspiration glistening on her skin.

"Wonderful! Brilliant! Exquisite!" There weren't enough adjectives to describe what people thought of Rani, but then a voice was whispering in Shanta's ear: "You dance beautifully, my dear. I should like you to be my pupil."

CHAPTER 4
The Chosen One

Shanta's face was flushed with the tremendous energy which had gripped her body and moved through her limbs. Her head was bowed when she heard the voice – an old, quavering, wrinkled voice, yet somehow harmonious, like a musical string. Shanta looked up slowly, her eye travelling from the floor, where sticking out from beneath the border of a sari, were a pair of thick boots. Up... up... her eyes travelled wonderingly. Up through the folds of the sari, and the drapes of a shawl until she found herself looking into the most ancient face she had ever seen, with skin as brown and creased as a walnut and with eyes as luminous and deep as moonlit waters.

"You are a dancer of the stone," murmured the old woman. She put her hands on Shanta's shoulders and pressed her fingers into Shanta's flesh, feeling her muscles and sinews. She moved her hands up her neck and to her head, moving it this way and that as if testing its strength.

"Yes, you have a body that is solid and strong but which will flow like water. I can teach you to be the best dancer in the world."

Shanta's brain was tumbling with thoughts. Somehow, she had known from the moment she had woken up that there was something different about this day. But how could she have known that today her entire future would be decided?

"Will you let me teach you?" asked the old lady, though her voice almost seemed to command it.

"I will... if my parents allow me."

"They will. I'll see to that." The old woman spoke with low confidence, and then moved away to be lost in the crowd.

"The old lady is Uma Rao!" Shanta's father spoke the name with awe and amazement. "She was once known as the finest dancer in India. Then, at the peak of her powers, she disappeared and no one ever saw her dance again. Even the Shankars didn't know who their lodger was until now."

"Just think of it!" Shanta's mother exclaimed with glee as they drove home after the party. "Uma Rao wants to teach *my* daughter. Not the fair, beautiful Rani Shankar, but *my* daughter, Shanta Biswas. Who would have thought that our dark little girl could be so special? Doesn't it just show you – money can't buy everything! Of course the old woman is very <u>eccentric</u> – I mean, did you notice she was wearing *boots*? Boots, I ask you. But the famous can afford to be eccentric, so who cares?" She turned to her daughter. "You could be famous and become rich and look after us in our old age. So I hope you'll work hard and do everything Uma Rao tells you, even if she makes you dance in boots too. That was the deal. She doesn't want any money. She just wants your complete obedience and dedication. You'll have to make some sacrifices."

Shanta smile quietly. At that moment she felt she would have given the old lady her soul in exchange for being able to dance.

So it was arranged, just as the old lady promised. Each Friday after school, Shanta was to cross the city and go for a lesson with Uma Rao in her basement flat in the Shankars' house.

The first day, she met her cousin on the steps. "Hello, Rani!" cried Shanta, so pleased to see her friend. But Rani did not return her smile. She looked strained and cold. "I've come for a dancing lesson. Aren't you pleased for me? It's what I always wanted," cried Shanta joyfully.

But Rani suddenly narrowed her eyes and spat out jealously, "Don't let it go to your head. You'll never be a dancer. Look at you – you're not pretty; you're just a lump. You'll never be as good as me, you can't be – not even with Uma Rao as a teacher!" She flounced indoors.

Shanta felt her heart grow so heavy she thought she would choke. Had she just made the first sacrifice – her friendship with Rani? She wanted to run after her and say, "Don't worry, Rani. I won't dance. I'd rather be your friend." But then she saw the old woman beckoning to her through the basement window, and she obeyed the silent command to come in.

Shanta entered a bare room. There were no carpets to cover the wooden floor boards. There were just a few cushions in one corner.

Uma Rao stood in the centre of the room. Her sari was drawn up and tucked in like loose trousers, which made her look even more bizarre in her boots. Yet she could never be a figure of fun. There was something about her too proud, too mysterious, too commanding for anyone to laugh. On the contrary, Shanta felt a tremor of anxiety as the sharp, needle-like gaze seemed to pierce her very thoughts.

The old lady bowed a formal namaste and Shanta did the same. Then the old lady took her behind a curtain and told her to change. She was to wear a pair of cotton, jodhpur-style trousers and a thin, close-fitting blouse, and there was a set of ankle bells for her to strap round each ankle. When Shanta emerged, tinkling with every step, she found that the blind boy who had played at the party was sitting on the cushions before a pair of tablas.

"Prem will play for you," said Uma Rao. "Although he is blind, his ears are better than most people's eyes. He will follow you and know your every mood and gesture just as if he could see."

So the dance classes began.

Week after week, Shanta crossed the city by bus to go to the old lady's basement flat for her lessons. But though Prem was always there, they never spoke to each other. Uma Rao would not allow talk. "Dance is the language of movement and expression," she would say. "We do not need speech." They would not dare to disobey her. Uma Rao didn't need speech to show her displeasure. One look from her told you instantly of her anger or her satisfaction.

So Shanta never had a chance to chat to Prem, for he was always there before she arrived, and he left before she did, to go back to his master. He had been dedicated to Mohan Datt since early childhood. From then on Mohan Datt had been father, mother, teacher and <u>guru</u> to him. One day, Prem would be a master. He too would have a disciple, and in this way, the skills of tabla-playing would be passed on from one generation to the next. But while he was a pupil, like Shanta, he had to show total obedience.

The old lady was very strict. It wasn't just that Shanta had to learn to dance, she also had to learn to pray and <u>meditate</u>. "Dancing is the same as praying," Uma Rao told her. Before every dancing lesson, Shanta had to sit cross-legged and concentrate. She had to learn to become the character she was dancing – whether it was a milkmaid or a goddess, a fish or a bird. Most of all, she had to dedicate herself body and soul to Lord Shiva. So, just as she had seen the tabla player kneeling before the altar, lighting incense sticks and murmuring prayers, Shanta did the same.

Week by week, month by month, Shanta got better and better. She knew it. She could feel it. She felt her body hardening up as her muscles strengthened; she felt her arms and fingers developing their own language, flowing more fluently than words from a mouth. As for her eyes... People who saw her dance said it was her eyes which made her special. They were so dark and deep; they could glow with love or flash with anger, they could quiver with expectation or drown with sorrow. Sometimes, to look into Shanta's eyes was like looking into the eyes of the Creator.

And wherever Shanta's mood and imagination took her, Prem, the blind boy, was there too. Rhythms which mirrored and echoed her dancing feet bubbled out from under his thin bony fingers as they moved over the surface of the drums; and though Prem and Shanta never spoke, it was as though he had become a part of her and understood her completely.

Every now and then Shanta had that dream of dancers in the rock, who leapt out of the stone to whirl through the night and then returned again to their <u>petrified</u> form. One night, one of the dancers was Uma Rao. But in Shanta's dream, Uma Rao wasn't old. She was young and strong and as beautiful as a goddess. Yet there was something terrible about her. Although she danced more magnificently than any other dancer, her face was drenched with tears, and then Shanta saw that, instead of bare, stamping feet, Uma Rao danced in boots.

One day, Uma Rao left the room briefly. Shanta took a chance and dared to talk to Prem. She wanted to ask the one question which had become an obsession and burned in her brain.

"Tell me," she whispered urgently and quickly. "Why does the old lady wear boots?"

"Why?" The boy's voice hung in the air like a long spider's thread. "I hope you'll never find out." he murmured. He could say no more as the old woman returned.

Then, one day, the master tabla player, Mohan Datt, came into Shanta's lesson. He didn't play, but sat cross-legged on the floor next to Prem and watched her, as on the day when he had played at Rani's thirteenth birthday. For an hour, he sat rigid, not saying a word. Shanta was aware of that same intense gaze, focusing on her like some spotlight, which followed her round and would not release her from its hold.

"Is this the Chosen One?" he asked in a low voice.

"She is," answered Uma Rao.

"Is she ready?"

"She is," nodded the old woman.

Then he and Uma Rao had a whispered conversation together in a language that Shanta didn't understand.

When the tabla player left, Uma Rao took Shanta's hand and said, "Shanta, the most important thing has happened. Something that every dancer yearns for. You have been invited to dance at a temple in India. It is a temple by the sea. It is very holy, and only a few chosen dancers in every lifetime are asked to dance there. The call has come for you. You must obey."

Shanta did not often look directly into her teacher's face except when she was learning a dance expression. Usually, her eyes were lowered with respect and she only spoke when spoken to. But there was something so strange in the way Uma Rao told her this news. The old lady's words told Shanta something which should make her the proudest and happiest girl in the world, yet there was a terrible sadness in Uma Rao's voice which made Shanta look wonderingly into her teacher's face.

"My dear..." said the old woman with unexpected tenderness. She stretched out a hand and gently touched Shanta's face. "If only..." She stopped and, as if afraid, turned abruptly away. "Get changed quickly." Her voice was harsh. "I will come home with you and tell your parents so that they can make plans immediately. I'll just get my shawl."

Once more, Shanta and Prem were briefly alone. But this time, it was Prem who made the first move. "So you are the Chosen One," he murmured, leaping to her side. His agile fingers moved up her arms and shoulders feeling their shape, then travelled like spider's legs, fluttering across her face, feeling her nose, her mouth, her cheeks, her chin – taking in all her features through his fingertips. Then his thin fingers gripped her arm, hurting her. "Listen to me," he said urgently.

Shanta was startled and couldn't help stepping back from the boy who stared up at her with sightless eyes.

"What is it?" she cried. "What's the matter?"

"The time has come. Now I must warn you. Please listen." He spoke rapidly, his voice quivering with anxiety.

"What do you mean, warn me? Warn me of what?"

"You are a Chosen One. That means that Uma Rao has chosen you to be a dancer for the goddess Kali. Now that she has taught you everything she knows, my master has arranged for you to dance in India in the temple by the sea. Only then will Uma Rao be freed from the curse. They will want you to dance on the terrace which the waves wash over when the tide comes in. But you must refuse. I warn you – refuse to dance there. For if you do, you will be cursed forever, just as the great Uma Rao was cursed."

"What do you mean, cursed? How?" cried Shanta.

But before the boy could answer, Uma Rao had reappeared wrapped in her shawl, telling Shanta to come.

"Will Prem be my tabla player?" Shanta asked.

"Oh no!" answered the old lady. "The master himself will play for you in the temple by the sea. But Prem will be there. A disciple is never apart from his master."

CHAPTER 5
Leaving Home

"I don't want to go!" Shanta remembered how she had forced those words from her lips, after Uma Rao had explained to her parents that she had been chosen to go and dance at the temple by the sea.

Her parents had reacted fiercely. "What do you mean, you don't want to go? Of course you do, silly girl. Didn't you hear what your teacher said?"

Oh yes, Shanta had heard the old lady's powerful words. "Only the very best dancer in any generation is asked to dance there," Uma Rao had said. "It is the highest honour, for your feet will stamp on the very stones on which Lord Shiva danced. His power will surge through the soles of your feet and you will dance like a god."

"Do I also dance for the goddess Kali?" Shanta dared to whisper.

Uma Rao looked started, briefly, as if a secret had been let out. Then she smiled stiffly and said, "Kali too, of course. Is she not Lord Shiva's consort?"

But Shanta also remembered the urgent warning of the blind boy, Prem. She had looked at Uma Rao's boots and longed to ask the question that now burned in her brain day and night – "Why do you wear boots? Is it to do with the curse?" But whenever she felt her courage rise and opened her mouth to ask, she would lose her nerve and sink back silent and angry with herself.

"You promised total dedication and obedience in exchange for dancing lessons," her father reminded her. "So if Uma Rao wants you to dance at this temple in India, then you must go – and that's an end of it," he said sternly, seeing Shanta's mouth open again to protest.

Shanta stood in her bedroom. Her eyes roamed lovingly round its walls. Pictures which had been there since the day she was born still hung there – pictures into whose depths she had often wandered in her imagination.

She picked up her oldest and dearest toy – a stuffed monkey, which she had had since she was a baby. Its fur was almost worn away in places from the hugging and kissing she had given it over the years. She looked into its glassy eyes and murmured, "I'm going to miss you." For Uma Rao had told Shanta that as she was going to India, she must put the past away and say farewell to her childhood.

Shanta looked up and saw herself in her wardrobe mirror. Was she no longer a child? How often she had stood in front of that mirror and examined herself. How often she had critically sighed over what she thought was her ugliness. "If only I could be as pretty as Rani," she used to think, "then perhaps Mum and Dad would love me more." How often she used to watch herself dancing. "When I grow up," she used to whisper. "When I grow up I want to be... I wish I could be a..." She would go right up to the mirror and press her face against her mirror image and whisper the word "dancer."

Ever since she became Uma Rao's pupil this greatest wish was no longer a secret. Everybody knew that Shanta Biswas was going to be a dancer. Now when she looked in the mirror and saw her dark face and arms, she felt special. She no longer wished she looked like Rani. Lord Shiva was dark; the dark, blue-throated god who danced the dance of creation.

Once when she had danced particularly well, she thought she heard Uma Rao murmur, "Yes... yes! You are truly a child of Shiva!"

She treasured those words, for Uma Rao hardly ever praised her – not like that. Usually, the most she would say was, "That's the way." Those words were enough, coming from someone who was so critical; and anyway, Shanta soon didn't need to be told when something had gone well. She could feel it in her own bones and see it by the small smile which would creep over Prem's face. Even though the boy could not see her, he could tell by every single other one of his senses; by the stamping of her feet and the excitement of the sung rhythms which echoed round the rooms from the voices of Shanta and her teacher. "Thakita-thakita-thakita-dhim! Thakita-thakita-thakita-dhim!"

Now she could look in her mirror and say, "When I grow up I *am* going to be a dancer."

This was her last day in her own room. Tomorrow, she was going to India. She knew she should be feeling great happiness. Isn't this what she had always dreamed of? Yet she was full of foreboding. Prem's words haunted her and filled her with a deep dread. She had tried to believe that her dancing was all for the good. But Rani had stopped being her friend. Even though Shanta went over to the Shankar house once a week for her dancing lessons, Rani no longer invited her in as she used to. Sometimes Shanta longed for the old days when she and Rani were friends.

When Rani knew that Shanta was going to be a dancer, it had made her jealous and competitive. "I'll show her!" she hissed spitefully. "I'll show that plain, dumpy little cousin of mine she isn't a patch on me." Rani had worked even harder at her dancing and was indeed becoming famous. She was often invited to give performances and had even danced on television.

But when Shanta told Rani that she was going to dance in India, in the temple by the sea, Rani had become rigid, as if her body had turned to stone. "It is you who should be going," cried Shanta, painfully aware of her cousin's jealousy. "I don't know why they chose me, when you are so beautiful and dance so wonderfully well."

"Oh, but I *am* going!" Rani had suddenly burst out triumphantly. "They have organized a tour of India for me, didn't you know? I'll be there too, don't you worry."

Shanta didn't know and wasn't sure if it was true, but she smiled generously and said, "Oh good!"

As the day of departure had drawn nearer, Shanta felt more and more disturbed. She had remembered Prem's warning. What had he meant by a curse? Shanta wished she could talk to him further and find out more, but she had never been left alone with him again, not for a single moment.

Suddenly, as she gazed at her mirror image, she thought she saw the room behind her open up into a fearful cave, where beyond, a great dark sea heaved and curled and looked as if it would hurl itself on top of her. She spun round, trembling with terror. He door flung open and her father came in.

"Shouldn't you be in bed, dearest?" he asked gently. "We have a big journey ahead of us tomorrow."

"Oh Dad!" She rushed into his arms and clung tightly. "I don't want to go," she whispered, and burst out sobbing.

"Hey, hey, hey! What is all this? What's got into you, Shanta? We're coming with you. This will be the most important dance of your life."

"Please, Dad, don't make me go to India tomorrow. I don't want to dance at this temple. Prem says..."

"What's all this nonsense? What does Prem say?" Shanta's mother burst in. "You don't want to go listening to that silly boy. After you have danced at the temple, you won't just have that sightless boy as your tabla player, you'll have the master himself. Now get to bed and get your beauty sleep."

"Beauty sleep?" Shanta cried even more. Before she had become Uma Rao's pupil, no one had thought her beautiful, not even her parents. But now, because they had been told that she would be a famous dancer, they all called her beautiful. Even more beautiful than Rani, they said.

Suddenly, she stopped crying. She dashed the tears from her eyes. Perhaps after all, this was part of her strange destiny and it would do no good to fight against it. "I'm ready to sleep," she said calmly, and firmly ushered her amazed parents from the room.

As Shanta lay in the darkness she stopped thinking about the future. She thought only of Prem. Dear blind Prem, who had never seen her; never judged whether her skin was too dark or her eyes too big or her body too stumpy. Somehow she felt no one else in the world really loved her as Prem did, and she was suddenly comforted. Whatever happened in India, at least Prem would be there – somewhere.

CHAPTER 6
The Night before

A wind swished across the surface of the ocean like a <u>scythe</u>. It chipped into the sea sending up flurries of white foam, and hewed out deep troughs into which fishing boats vanished, then reappeared, poised, almost as if they would fly from the sharp-ridged crests of the waves.

The farmers straightened their backs, looked briefly out to sea and wondered if they were in for a storm. They did not envy their brothers, the fishermen, whose sails they could see dotted over a wide area, still far from the shore.

A priest stood in his <u>saffron</u> robe on the partly submerged terrace of the temple, holding a holy thread and sacred beads. He chanted prayers and tossed marigolds and bits of coconut into the rising tide. "Soon, soon!"

He stretched out his arms. "Soon, O Kali, we will offer you another dancer – the best we can find – to glorify your temple." His words mingled with the screeching of the seagulls that wheeled and soared and pecked at the waves.

Back in the village, the people had been

in a frenzy of preparations for the Kali Festival which had come round once more. Using sugar cane and bamboo and dried leaves, and moulding it all together with clay, they gradually built a huge black effigy of the goddess Kali.

This year, the priest had told them, was a special year – a propitious year. They would be offering another dancer to Kali to placate her anger and save them from any more earthquakes. So they had built their effigy of Kali even taller than usual, and the villagers had donated some of their finest cloth and jewellery to adorn this fearsome goddess. They placed the figure on a chariot and she towered twenty feet above them – suddenly seeming divine, even though they had made her with their own hands.

It was the night before the full moon. The night before Shanta would dance at the temple by the sea. As the giant orange sun sank into the ocean, they raised an oil-filled lamp on to a high pole, and through the enveloping darkness, those fishermen not yet home fixed their eyes on the shining light and made for the shore. All around, glimmering from every household in the village, were oil-drenched wicks burning in honour of dead ancestors.

"Is she here?" the priest asked Mohan Datt. The two men stood among the walls of the temple, where the ocean heaved at their feet and the stone people crowded round them looking as if they would leap out of the rock and join in the festivities that throbbed through the darkness.

The master tabla player nodded. "We have brought you the best. Tomorrow, here on the temple terrace at sunset, she will dance and we will offer her to Kali. Then Uma Rao will be free."

In the shadows, the blind boy listened and his tears overflowed.

Shanta had never been to India before, yet she was told this was home. She stood at the window of the simple brick house on the edge of the village and gazed out across the brown tilled fields. The bullock pulling the plough had followed the lie of the land; it coiled in swirls among mango groves and clumps of banana trees, and cut furrows which ran right to the very edge of the sea.

A full moon was rising, and already there were the sounds of pipes and drums and chanting voices, and children squealing and laughing, and garlands of bells jingling round the necks of horses and bullocks. It seemed that every living creature was intent on celebrating the Kali Festival. People had made new clothes to wear, decorated their houses, painted their animals, threaded hundreds of garlands of flowers – so that the air was <u>cloying</u> with the smell of marigolds and jasmine and tube lilies. They had lit their oil lamps and placed them on their roofs and balconies and verandas, shining as bright as day.

Shanta could hear the excitement and happiness all around her, yet she felt terribly afraid. She could see Prem standing at the edge of the field, his face turned into the wind which blew in from the sea. She knew that he too was afraid. If only she knew why.

She was alone in her room with instructions to pray and meditate in preparation for her dance at the temple. But she couldn't control her thoughts or her fears, though she tried over and over again, kneeling before an image of Shiva. She remembered that she had first glimpsed the master tabla player kneeling before Kali, not Shiva. To whom should she pray? She lit several incense sticks, trying to let the thin smoky smell invade her mind and help her to concentrate on her performance, but it was hopeless. Over and over again, she went to the window and looked out across the sea, wishing she was back home in her own room in England. Why, oh why had she ever wanted to dance?

A distant movement caught her eye. She saw Uma Rao taking a back path which led down to a lonely part of the shore. She had fresh clothes draped over her arm, so Shanta knew she was going to bathe. In an instant, Shanta realized that this was her only chance to satisfy her curiosity. Without any further thought, she slipped out of her room, across a back veranda and down on to the same path which led to the sea.

It was a gradual track which took the old lady gently down to the shore.

Moonlight and sunlight together glittered on the waves like gold and silver coins. Without removing her clothes, Uma Rao waded out into the sea. Then, when she was waist deep, she unwound her sari, took off her blouse and submerged herself completely, the loose cloth swirling around her. Then Shanta nearly cried out with terror and excitement. Uma Rao dipped under the water again and removed her boots. One by one, she tossed them onto the shore, then threw up her arms and began to chant prayers.

Shanta crept as near as she dared and hid behind a rock, just a few yards from where the old lady had placed her new dry clothes. She would have to come out and then, Shanta knew, this would be the moment when she would see the great dancer's feet at last.

Uma Rao's prayers seemed to go on for ever, then suddenly, they stopped. The old lady turned and seemed to look straight at her. Shanta recoiled out of sight, her heart almost leaping out of her chest with fear. Had she been seen? She heard faint splashes, as Uma Rao waded ashore. Pressing her body into the curve of the rock, Shanta risked another peep. It only took one look. One dreadful look. She fell back, fainting, stuffing her hand into her mouth to stop her crying out. At last, she had seen what she had craved to see. She had seen Uma Rao's feet.

CHAPTER 7
The Dance of the Temple

Shanta's mother helped her to dress. The best tailor had stitched Shanta a magnificent dancing skirt and trousers in scarlet and gold silk. Her long black hair was plaited and coiled with jasmine and pearls, her eyes were outlined in black charcoal and her skin brushed with a pale powder which made her gleam. The palms of her hands and her feet were intricately patterned with <u>henna</u> and Shanta was bejewelled – she was spangled with jewels like the night sky. Clusters of pearl dangled from her ears; they were linked by a thin chain of gold to a glittering diamond stud which gleamed on her nose. Necklaces of emeralds and rubies entwined her throat and descended in a criss-cross of gold chains across her midriff. Gold and silver rings flashed on her fingers and toes; the bracelets on her arms and the bells round her ankles tinkled with every movement.

"For goodness sake, girl, look a bit more cheerful. Your face is as glum as if you were going to a funeral. This is the most important day of your life," her mother begged her. "From now on, they will treat you like a goddess."

But it was as if Shanta – the Self – had vacated her body and left an empty shell.

When she was finally led from the house, people thought Shanta was in a trance, for her face was as expressionless as a doll's. She was held by her father on one side and Mohan Datt, the tabla player, on the other, and they seemed almost to carry her along.

A fantastic procession had formed, with jogging musicians and excited families, decorated bullocks and finely groomed horses. They brought out the elephant from the temple – all painted and garlanded and carrying four or five young boys, who supported a tall effigy of a dancing Lord Shiva. Young, strong-muscled men with huge, fringed umbrellas ran alongside a chariot which was completely entwined and draped with flowers. On top of the chariot, swaying as if she were alive, was the great black figure of Kali. If special disciples had been chosen to pull her along, you could hardly see them, for everyone wanted to help – men, women and children, the young and the old, the pregnant, the weak, the sick, the crippled and the blind. They all wanted to touch, to see, to just be within Kali's shadow so that some slight speck of her power might fall upon them and bring them good fortune.

They made a space for Shanta behind Kali's chariot. No one crowded round her. Instead, they fell back with awe, whispering and pointing, with a strange dread on their faces.

"Is she going to dance at the temple by the sea?" asked a child's high voice.

"Ssssh!" They dared not answer.

The temple seemed big enough to absorb everyone. They swarmed all over it; up the terraces, along the walls, among the ruins, up and down its many steps; some even into the sea itself, slithering and slipping on the seaweedy boulders.

But into the innermost sanctum, into the darkest heart of the temple, they led Shanta. The only light came from a low sacred flame, tended by two saffron-clad priests, who softly chanted and tossed holy water and waved sticks of rich incense. The light flickered over two giant figures carved out of the rock.

Only then did Shanta seem to come alive. She turned to the figure on whom the dawn rays fell each morning. Her eyes travelled up its immense torso, till she found herself gazing at the most beautiful, powerful face she had ever seen. Lord Shiva gazed down at her out of the rock. Two eyes, though carved in stone, seemed to glimmer with a life force. The third eye, in the middle of his forehead, was half-closed, not wanting to look upon the faithful in case its power should destroy them.

"Oh please, Lord Shiva, save me!" Shanta sent up a silent prayer. "I only wanted to dance – that's all. I don't want to be the best or the greatest. I don't want fame and fortune. I only want to dance to make me happy." She would not turn and face the other figure, Kali, who was equally huge, whose fearsome shape seemed ready to leap out of the rock and devour her.

The master tabla player nudged Shanta to approach the sacred fire. He took her hand and passed it three times through the flame, while prayers rose and echoed round the cave. Then a priest pressed his thumb into a mixture of ash and dung and <u>vermilion</u> and smeared it on to her forehead. He sprinkled holy water over her head and feet and then blessed her.

Uma Rao stood in the shadow of one of the columns, merging into it like a statue. The master tabla player left Shanta and sat before his tablas which had been placed on the terrace, whose stones were already being lapped by the incoming tide. The blind boy sat beside him, strumming the tanpura. Its note droned and reverberated as if awakening the souls of the dead. As Shanta walked out to take her position in the centre of the terrace, Prem lifted his face towards her as if seeing her with his blind eyes.

"Dance now. Dance, my child," murmured Uma Rao. "Dance with the spirit of Lord Shiva. Be our sacrifice. Dance to placate the anger of the goddess Kali. Dance to free me from the curse."

The tabla began its beat. Shanta stamped a foot and picked up the rhythm. She caught the eye of the tabla player, just as she had done – was it a lifetime ago? – at Rani's birthday party. He seemed to hypnotize her, and she felt her whole body giving in to the need to dance and dance and dance.

"Ahhaaah!" She heard the ecstatic sighs around her as her magic began to work.

A wave rose up and fell on the terrace steps, part of it swirling towards her, but just receding before it touched her feet.

Prem's finger faltered on the strings and the hum of the drone was interrupted. But Shanta hardly noticed. She was dancing better than she had ever danced in her life and she never wanted to stop. "Thakka-dhimi-thakka-jhanu, thakka-dhimi-thakka-jhanu!" The tabla player's voice rang out over the beat of the drums. Her feet stamped in answer, her eyes gleamed and flashed out their messages.

Another wave rose and fell. This time, only a step backwards saved Shanta's feet from being submerged. Prem laid aside the tanpura and stood up. Everyone was in a trance. He heard the next wave coming from far off. He felt it gathering itself together, coiling up its head like a cobra, poised and ready to dart out across the terrace. The tabla player beat the drums even harder. Shanta leapt towards the sea as if to embrace the wave and at that moment, with a great cry, Prem threw himself upon her and dragged her out of the temple.

The drum beat hardly stopped for breath, for in that instant, another dancer sprang into Shanta's place on the terrace stones. "Let me, let me dance!" she cried. The tabla player nodded and smiled, as Rani picked up the rhythms and gave herself body and soul to the dance.

The wave had waited – as a cobra waits to strike – but now it broke, and in its fall, it was as if it released the piteous voices of a million tormented souls. It swept across Rani's feet. Wave after wave rose and fell, till soon the terrace was submerged in the sea. But Rani danced on until the waves lifted her from the ground and her feet could stamp no more.

EPILOGUE

After the fateful day at the temple, Rani Shankar became known as the most fabulous dancer in the whole world. Rani danced before the greatest – in all the grand theatres. She was adored, as no one else was adored – though just a few said that to see Shanta Biswas dance, accompanied by her blind tabla player, was to see a child of the gods.

Then one day, Rani disappeared. It was exactly ten years after she had danced in the temple by the sea. For a while, people were distraught and searched for her high and low. But then they forgot Rani, just as they had forgotten Uma Rao, and they turned instead to Shanta and wondered why they hadn't thought her the greatest all along.

More years went by, till one day Shanta went to a theatre, out of curiosity, to see a young dancer perform. It was said that this young girl was destined to be the finest dancer of her generation. As the child danced, Shanta noticed her teacher, a woman, standing in the shadows of the stage, watching intently. With a gasp, Shanta hurriedly left her seat and made her way backstage. She was sure she knew the teacher and wanted desperately to talk to her. She rushed along dark corridors and finally came up on the other side of the stage from the woman.

As the marvellous child whirled about between them in the spotlight, the two women met each other's tragic gaze. Even from that distance, Shanta saw the boots poking out from beneath the simple sari. Then she knew. Her heart burst with pity as she raised her eyes again and dared to look into Rani's face. Slowly, Rani bent and took off her boots. Shanta knew what she would see. It would be the same as when she had spied Uma Rao coming out of the ocean. For a moment, she turned away in dread, but then, her eyes brimming with tears, Shanta looked back to her cousin and childhood friend and saw the feet of stone, the same hard, grey, granite stone of the temple by the sea.

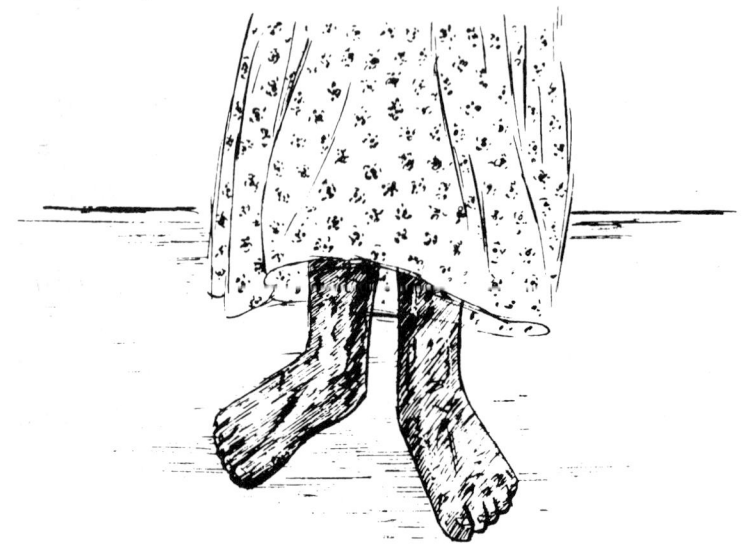

Shanta never saw her own teacher, Uma Rao, ever again – at least not as a living human being. It was as though she had never existed. But one day, when Shanta was nearly old herself, she and Prem found themselves travelling near the village with its temple by the sea.

"Stay here, Prem, at the rest house and bathe," Shanta said gently. "I want to take a walk and stretch my legs after our long journey."

Prem sighed. He knew where she was going, but he didn't try to stop her.

She wandered along a dusty track which ran between the rice fields and soon reached the lonely, grey, granite stones of the temple. The rise and fall of the waves and the calling gulls mingled with ghostly voices, vibrating strings and hammering drums. She touched the rock face, running her fingers over the carved figures of dancers who almost seemed to turn and watch her as she moved slowly past them.

Suddenly she stopped and stared. One figure caught her eye. It was a beautiful dancer sculpted out of one of the columns which held up the roof over the terrace, where Shanta had danced on that fateful day. A life-sized statue of a woman gazed down on her, just a little taller than she was. The woman's feet were raised in a mighty stamp – Shanta could see all the toes spread out with energy – and so perfectly carved they could have been living feet. The arms were raised as if gracefully beckoning. Then Shanta looked into her face. Perhaps spray from the sea had been swept in by the wind and gathered in all the delicate ridges and lines of the sculpture; but as Shanta looked into the stone face of Uma Rao, she saw tears trickling slowly down those hard, grey cheeks.

Nearby, on the great stone frieze, behind Uma Rao and the line of dancers, was a space in the rock waiting to be filled.

Glossary

p. 5 meagre	very little, not very good
p. 6 effigy	a hand-made religious statue
p. 7 sari	a woman's dress made by draping a long strip of cloth around the body
p. 6 edifice	a grand building
p. 8 cosmos	the universe
p. 8 annihilated	completely destroyed
p. 13 Divali	a Hindu festival of lightdedicated to the goddess Lakshmi.
p. 13 caravan	a procession
p. 16 shalwar kameez	a kind of loose trouser suit worn by men and women in India
p. 17 tabla drums	pairs of drums used in traditional Indian music
p. 18 torso	the main part of the body between the neck and the legs.
p. 22 samosas	pastry triangles containing vegetables or meat
p. 22 rouge	blusher: make up to make the cheeks look pink
p. 22 tilak	a red dot worn by Hindus on their foreheads. It is a sign of welcome and wisdom.

p. 24 incense	scented powder or oils often burned in religious ceremonies
p. 27 tanpura	a stringed instrument used in traditional Indian music.
p. 27 drone	a single note played in the background of a piece of music
p. 27 namaste	a formal greeting in which you put your hands together, bow slightly and say "namaste"
p. 34 eccentric	behaving in an unusual way; unconventional
p. 38 guru	a special teacher
p. 38 meditate	to train the mind to concentrate; thinking about religious matters
p. 42 petrified	turned to stone
p. 47 consort	a wife or husband
p. 56 scythe	a long curved knife for cutting crops
p. 56 saffron	a yellow or orange colour
p. 57 propitious	fortunate, promising good things
p. 57 placate	make peace with
p. 60 cloying	too rich or sweet
p. 64 henna	a brown/orange plant dye
p. 68 vermilion	a brilliant red dye